It's a Sunflower!

¡Es un girasol!

Elisa Peters

Traducción al español:
Eduardo Alamán

PowerKiDS & **Editorial Buenas Letras**™
press.
New York

For Hannah Kang

Published in 2009 by The Rosen Publishing Group, Inc.
29 East 21st Street, New York, NY 10010

Copyright © 2009 by The Rosen Publishing Group, Inc.

First Edition

Editor: Amelie von Zumbusch
Book Design: Greg Tucker
Photo Researcher: Jessica Gerweck

Photo Credits: All images by Shutterstock.com.

Library of Congress Cataloging-in-Publication Data

Peters, Elisa.
   [It's a sunflower! Spanish & English]
   It's a sunflower! = ¡Es un girasol! / Elisa Peters ; traducción al español, Eduardo Alamán. –
1st ed.
       p. cm. – (Everyday wonders = Maravillas de todos los días)
   Added t.p. title: ¡Es un girasol!
   Includes index.
   ISBN 978-1-4358-2523-9 (library binding)
   1. Sunflowers–Life cycles–Juvenile literature. I. Title. II. Title: ¡Es un girasol!
   QK495.C74P4818 2009
   583'.99–dc22

                                                             2008004051

Manufactured in the United States of America

Web Sites: Due to the changing nature of Internet links, PowerKids Press and Editorial Buenas Letras have developed an online list of Web sites related to the subject of this book. This site is updated regularly. Please use this link to access the list:
www.powerkidslinks.com/wonder/sunflower/

Contents/Contenido

This beautiful flower is
a sunflower.

Esta hermosa flor es un girasol.

Sunflowers have yellow **petals**.

Los girasoles tienen **pétalos**
de color amarillo.

Sunflowers are very tall.

Los girasoles son muy altos.

Sunflower plants start out
as **seedlings**.

Los girasoles comienzan como
plantas de **semillero**.

Seedlings grow tall. They form **buds** that open into flowers.

Los semilleros crecen muy alto. Luego, forman **brotes** que se convierten en flores.

⑬

Seeds form in the center
of the sunflower.

En el centro de los girasoles
se forman **semillas**.

In time, sunflower seeds
turn black.

Con el tiempo, las semillas de
los girasoles se hacen negras.

Birds like to eat sunflower seeds.

A los pájaros les gusta comer las semillas de los girasoles.

Lots of people eat these yummy seeds, too.

Muchas personas comen estas ricas semillas.

Farmers grow sunflowers and gather the plants' seeds.

Los agricultores siembran girasoles y recolectan sus semillas.

Words to Know/Palabras que debes saber

bud
(el) brote

petals
(los) pétalos

seedlings
(los) semilleros

seeds
(las) semillas

Index

Índice